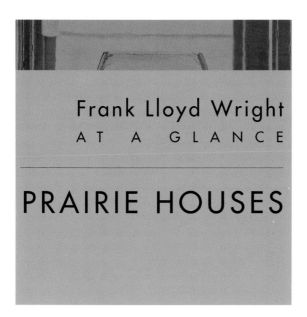

# Frank Lloyd Wright
## AT A GLANCE

# PRAIRIE HOUSES

# Frank Lloyd Wright
## AT A GLANCE

# PRAIRIE HOUSES

### Abby Moor

PRC

For Jens

This edition first published in 2002 by
PRC Publishing Ltd,
64 Brewery Road, London N7 9NT
A member of the Chrysalis Group plc

Distributed in the U.S. and Canada by:
Sterling Publishing Co., Inc.
387 Park Avenue South
New York, NY 10016

ISBN 1 85648 631 1

Printed and bound in China

Page iii:  There is a strong influence of the arts of Japan in much of Wright's
work of the Prairie period. He had visited Japan in 1905, and was a collector of
Japanese prints.

ACKNOWLEDGMENTS: The publisher wishes to thank Simon Clay for taking all
the photography in this book, including the photographs on the front and back
covers, with the following exceptions:

© Matt Phalen for the photographs on pages 64 and  65;

© Bettmann/Corbis for the photograph on the back cover (top).

# CONTENTS

# INTRODUCTION

Frank Lloyd Wright (1869–1959) was born in the American Midwestern state of Wisconsin in 1867. After studying engineering he left for the urban metropolis of Chicago, Illinois, where he first took a job in the office of the architect J.L. Silsbee. He soon, however, entered the innovative and prestigious architectural firm of Adler and Sullivan, and quickly became the practice's principal draftsman. As Dankmar Adler (1844–1900) and Louis Henry Sullivan (1856–1924) were chiefly concerned with their commercial commissions, Wright quickly took charge of most of the firm's projects for residential buildings. He remained with Adler and Sullivan until 1893 when he left the practice to establish an independent architectural practice in the Chicago suburb of Oak Park, where many of his finest Prairie houses were built. For the rest of his long career he continued to focus primarily on refining the principles of domestic architecture, designing over 1000 private residences throughout the United States.

During his career, Wright's productivity was enormous, and the pace with which he was able to design was already established in these early, independent years. By 1900, he had designed over 50 individual homes. His early architectural style was formative and eclectic, reflecting influences of the American revivalist architect Henry Hobson Richardson (1838–86), as well as of the American Domestic Revival, or shingle style so popular for houses of medium scale during the decades of the 1870s and 1880s.

However, it was the so-called Prairie Style emerging out of the Chicago School of architects that impressed upon the young Wright the architectural values of regionalism deriving from the Arts and Crafts movement. The Chicago School included Sullivan as well as two architects who had trained with him, the Scottish-born George Grant Elmslie, and George Washington Maher (1864–1926). Their values stressed the use of conventional ornament based upon the abstraction of nature, the moral importance of employing local materials in an "honest" fashion, and the development of an "organic" approach to design, which sought to bind a building to its site and its distinctive, regional landscape. The new Prairie Style buildings were thought

RIGHT: One of the many leaded and stained-glass designs for interior lighting in Wright's Prairie houses. This example was designed for the Susan Lawrence Dana house, Illinois, around 1903, and shows such a high degree of "conventionalization" of plant motifs that the final result has become remarkably abstracted.

LEFT: Prairie School architects, including Wright, situated the hearth at the center of the home to serve as the heart of family life in both practical and symbolic terms.

to embody these qualities by virtue of their integrated, organic approach to design. The Prairie School architects, including Wright, also shared a vision of contemporary architecture freed from any historicist reference—that is to say, any certain reliance upon identifiable styles of the past. They favored the use of broad, long and often drawn-out architectural forms, which almost imperceptibly merged with the Midwestern prairie's own long, low horizon.

From 1901 until he left for Europe in 1909, Wright developed his remarkable personal expression of this vernacular American building type. When he left Chicago in 1909 with Mamah Cheney, the wife of one of his patrons, his associates in his architectural practice followed through with the outstanding commissions. Wright's Prairie house period is generally thought of as dating from between 1901 and around 1910. Wright conceived of the residential Prairie house as a somewhat statuesque low-lying entity with parts

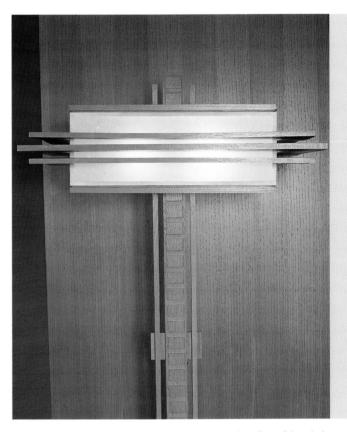

of clear geometric derivation, and a deeply overhanging roof and pronounced chimney. The effect of the whole was to impart the image of the domestic residence as shelter. His innovations pushed somewhat beyond those of other Prairie School architects in making structure itself an expression of his "organic" theories. Wright held that beauty in a building was the natural outcome of a clear statement by the architect of simple and harmonious relationships. All elements of a building should be designed with economy according to the natural laws of geometry and the honest use of materials. Beauty could not be enforced upon a building. Nor could it result from disguise of any sort. Rather, architectural beauty was a reflection of the harmony that arose between the sympathetic integration of plan, site, form, and materials; in short, from an organic approach to design.

In his 1932 *An Autobiography*, Wright famously proposed that "pure design is abstraction of nature-elements in purely geometric terms." He had always been fascinated by relationships between geometry

ABOVE: The majority of Wright's Prairie houses date from between 1901 and 1910. However, a few later houses, such as the Herbert F. Johnson house (also known as "Wingspread") of 1937, are stylistically so closely related to Wright's original Prairie phase that they are generally considered to be a mature continuation of that idiom.

and nature. The Froebel educational blocks he had played with as a child may have in part nourished this lifelong interest. For Wright, the relationship of a building to its site was the same thing as the relationship between geometry and nature. Geometry arose from nature, and was in essence nature abstracted.

Wright proposed that the horizontal line was "the line of domesticity." His more elaborate Prairie houses tend to have a strong horizontal presence, the mass of the house seeming to grow upward and outward from a governing

LEFT: Main interior features, such as balustrades, stairwells, ceiling beams, and even furnishings and lighting (as shown here) were designed by Wright to express the very principles of the Prairie house in their play of geometric forms, and their strong vertical and horizontal rhythms.

horizontal axis. This lumbering, earth-bound movement can be juxtaposed to an understated vertical patterning—sometimes as simple as the placement of rows of windows—across the surface of facade walls. In many of Wright's Prairie structures the horizontal axis governs the plan. It can be perceived as a long line beginning at one end with an open veranda. This then runs through the center of the house, terminating in, for example, a porte-cochere (a porch without a balustrade which could accommodate wheeled vehicles) at the opposite end. This refined balancing of architectural forms against one another, on either side of a dominant axis, is only one of the factors that lent Wright's designs such sophisticated intricacy.

Wright also had a strong sense of the picturesque possibilities of architecture. He developed a visual vocabulary based upon combinations of different basic geometric forms—at this early stage, usually squares and rectangles. Many of his better known Prairie houses are of the long and spreading sort, while others are elegantly square or plainly rectangular. At first, Wright rarely varied from his usual L-shaped or cruciform (in the shape of a cross) ground plans. Both of these had the advantage of decidedly separating the more intimate from the more public domains within the home, and allowed Wright to position certain types of rooms on one or more levels of a specific wing. But even in the simpler, rectangular Prairie Style dwellings he often interjected a subtle, but deliberate asymmetrical arrangement of bold shapes. These adjustments invested the structural mass of his houses with the quality of a rocky outcropping viewed against a hypothetical horizon, and demonstrated his passion for the purity of architectural expression.

Form, for Wright, also took on a symbolic meaning. Vertical planes, in the guise of the balustrade wall or the facade wall itself, served to insulate the private space of the home from the public areas outside. The Robie house, the Willits house, and the Heurtley house are only some of the properties where both the direct view of the house and access to it are guarded by a series of exterior retaining walls and parapets that reach forward from the house toward the street or drive. These veranda walls, balconies, or parapets delineate what is "outside" the private realm of the family home from what belongs within the family domain even if it exists on the exterior of the house proper, for example a veranda surrounded by a low retaining wall. These houses, therefore, can also comprise a series of transitional spaces in the form of "ramparts," which must be traversed in order to gain access. In the same sense, the house itself is raised above the level of the ground on a stylobate—a cement step or foundation—which is also part of an outside ring of structural devices meant to control penetration into the sanctuary. Living spaces are actually not sited at ground level, but raised above. The most intimate spaces, the bedrooms, are consistently located on the upper floors, isolated from the activity of the rest of the house and from outside noise, not only in accordance with Victorian tradition, but also symbolically protected beneath the shelter of the massive eaves of the Prairie roof.

For Wright, the plan of a home could not be dictated by the arbitrary rules of style. Rather, the layout of a building resulted exclusively from the arrangement of rooms inside and the interrelationships between them. Rooms situated around the centre of a horizontal axis, such as the living and dining areas, often signified the symbolic "backbone" of this type of Wrightian Prairie house. Outside, the sprawl of Wright's larger residences was accommodated by sites large enough to allow the building to move away from its central core in at least two directions.

The same philosophy of organic design governed Wright's Prairie house interiors. In fact, he argued that the true nature of any building begins with its interior spaces, and that the exterior will necessarily reveal, rather than disguise, the organisation of rooms. All interior features were intended to underscore the symbolic meaning of the house as a private dwelling. The dining and living areas were of equal importance in Wright's Prairie houses. Clustered together at the center of the plan, these rooms played the most significant role in the ritual of the nuclear family. They were also semi-public spaces where guests were invited to socialise, join in the activities of the family or participate in family ceremony. These comparatively traditional, insular and ultimately conservative values did much to insure a formal distribution of functional space in Wright's Prairie houses, especially where these homes were commissioned by the well-to-do, who maintained strict distinctions between private and social spaces within the home.

Dell Upton has observed that Wright's insistent centralisation of the hearth in the Prairie house plan was little more than a continuation of Victorian conventions surrounding the fireplace as an "emblem of togetherness." Upton has also argued that Wright conventionally relegated staff quarters to otherwise impractical spaces located behind the kitchen and carefully insulated from the family's private and social spaces by the imposition of, for example, storage areas such as closets and pantries. Clearly, despite the architectural experimentation and innovation that Wright's Prairie houses genuinely represent, sociologically they signify the domestic conventions of their patronage.

The Arts and Crafts Movement which arose almost simultaneously in Britain and the United States prescribed the interdisciplinary role of the architect as not only a builder and draftsman, but as a designer of

ABOVE: Many of Wright's Prairie houses, such as the Susan Lawrence Dana house, are part of an extensive complex of horizontal levels and vertical planes, in which low running walls create an almost maze-like configuration buttressing the home from the world outside.

ABOVE: Wright's design solution was to view all details of a building as the product of a single, independent mind, including minor decorative and symbolic motifs.

fixtures and fittings, furnishings, textiles, and stained glass as well. This approach stressed the importance of the complete integration in the design of the building with the design of its furnishings. Wright excelled in this role with more sheer brilliance than perhaps any other late-Victorian, early twentieth-century American architectural practitioner, except the brothers Charles Sumner Greene (1868–1957) and Henry Mather Greene (1870–1954), whose work was concentrated on the West Coast in California. As practitioners, they all shared a belief in the indivisibility of the arts as the animating force behind the production of architecture.

For Wright, chief amongst the "arts" of architecture was stained glass, because it was a medium that could by its very nature be fully integrated into architectural structure, and was therefore well suited to implement the notion of organic unity in the Prairie house. Like most practitioners influenced by the Arts and Crafts Movement, both in America

and Britain, Wright loathed the prospect of having to lodge a client's own incongruous furnishings within his carefully articulated architectural environments. Designing furniture for many of his architectural commissions allowed him to fully develop the concept of a homogeneous interior. Beginning in the Prairie houses, Wright integrated built-in settles and other seating, bookcases, sideboards, shelves and cupboards, closets, and inset lighting into the fabric of the building, in addition to designing free-standing furniture and lighting, rugs, vases, and murals for specific houses.

Wright's garden design for the Prairie house was developed along both romantic and practical lines, with combinations of natural habitat, grass lawns, planted beds, and an emphasis on evergreens of horizontal habit positioned around the patio or veranda. His aim of creating complete harmony between a building and its site extended to the treatment of the site itself.

ABOVE: Wright developed his own distinctive ornamental vocabulary. With it he strove to unify the interior and exterior of each Prairie house through its decorative detailing. Through his "organic" method, he unified structural and aesthetic elements into a single entity. This would then express the architectural beauty arising from the simple and harmonious relationships within his work.

Wright's approach to his materials in part echoed the British Arts and Crafts idealist, John Ruskin, whose authority influenced designers to look directly to nature for both instruction and inspiration. He employed stone masonry or red brick frequently in his Prairie designs, using the material with intention precisely where and when he desired it. In Wright's thinking, the textural integrity of any construction material should be allowed to speak symbolically and structurally for itself, as part of an overall organic design strategy.

Nevertheless, Wright's consistent experimentation with cement stucco from the early Prairie houses onward was a comparatively new development in American architecture. His predecessors had preferred the use of half-timbered surfaces for the exterior of domestic residences, in imitation of the English Tudor style, or the traditional and simple board-and-batten. Although the use of plaster was relatively common in the interior of a house, even there its inherent surface qualities were disguised by the Victorian preference for wallpaper as a way of adding patterning; essentially, interior wall surfaces were seen as the realm of two-dimensional ornamentation, often illusionistic and pictorial.

On both the interior and exterior of his Prairie houses, Wright exploited the natural properties of stucco. The interiors were plastered smooth for a precise and refined surface texture, and the addition of coarser sand produced a hardier texture for the exterior. The implication was an aesthetic movement away from European-derived tradition in favor of construction materials that reflected vernacular practices of the American continent. Stucco was rarely, if ever, used in "sophisticated," architect-designed residential architecture before Wright's promotion of it as a more natural material. Aesthetic considerations aside, cement stucco was also a less expensive building material, noticeably reducing the cost of the "designed" home in comparison to one in which brick or common stone masonry were employed. Cement stucco also had the advantage of being easily molded to any plastic surface plane, and because of this has been viewed by numerous Wrightian scholars as a precedent for Wright's subsequent experimentation with poured concrete. Both chemical compositions allowed Wright to realize broad and very even surfaces along extended geometric planes, emphasizing the forms and volumes of his buildings above all else. In this approach, Wright was very much part of the modernist agenda of early twentieth-century architecture, moving away from the limitations of traditional construction practices in favor of the new freedoms possible for architectural design.

# CASE STUDIES

# SUSAN LAWRENCE DANA HOUSE

Constructed: 1902
Address: Dana-Thomas House State Historic Site, 301 East Lawrence Avenue,
Springfield, Illinois. Tel: 217-782-6776
Hourly tours Wednesday through Sunday 9am to 4pm.

The Susan Lawrence Dana house is considered the most exhaustive surviving example of Wright's Prairie house aesthetic. It comprises 35 rooms and was originally commissioned by the affluent socialite Susan Dana as a remodeling of her existing family home dating from 1868. Traces of the original family home survive in the hearth, the foundation, and some walls to conform with the patron's instructions. A great deal of documentation on the designing and building of the house also survives, allowing its history to be studied in some detail.

The plan is a double cross-axis, and the house comprises a series of different levels, including interior viewing balconies. On the ground floor there were ancillary rooms, such as the private library, billiard, and bowling rooms. Above this the more public areas of the house open up in vistas that run through the dining and living rooms, the double-height reception area, and the gallery. It is the first of Wright's elevations to incorporate a living area that is two floors in height. Susan Dana remained in the property until 1928, and the site was subsequently bought by Thomas Publishing in 1944, then by the State of Illinois in 1981. It was completely restored in 1990.

RIGHT: The Susan Lawrence Dana house is constructed of Roman brick, imported from England, of a warm golden gray hue which gives a visual lightness in contrast to the solid forms of masonry. Even outside the house, Wright coordinated a flow of space that alternates between open, expansive areas and smaller, more compressed ones, such as those containing outside steps.

RIGHT: The entryway to the Dana house is one of the most frequently reproduced images of any of Wright's Prairie residences. It consists of a series of brick planes, which are situated forward and back in relation to the honey-colored banding. Massive brick and cement plinths guard each side of the door, which is deeply recessed into a shallow darkened vault beneath the slightly flattened semicircular arch of the entrance. The elaborate design of this feature has ritualistic overtones, and responds to the patron's need for an entryway of strong formal character.

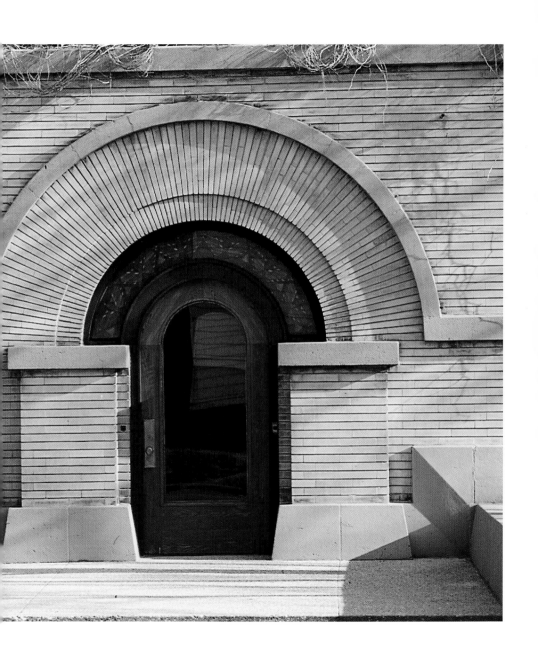

LEFT: The deeply cut eaves of the gabled roof are bound along their contours with intricately textured copper guttering, which flares upward and out at the corners. The profile of the house against the sky has an ancient and exotic quality.

RIGHT: Upper reaches of the facade are covered with a frieze of molded plaster panels that produce a richness of exterior surface texture unequaled until Wright implemented his "textile-block" house designs in California many years later.

ABOVE: Wright designed more than 450 examples of art glass for the Dana House. These included the opulent windows, and approximately 200 light fixtures and lamps in various forms, freestanding and in-built. His patterns were based upon two principal motifs, the abstracted sumac plant and the butterfly. The presence of leaded art glass windows replaced the need for other forms of window treatment. The glass acted as a form of drapery that filtered ample but diffused natural light through its refined patterns and colors.

RIGHT: Inside the Dana house, Wright was able to devise a series of intimate, yet very sizeable spaces. The warm architectural qualities of the rooms are highlighted by his use of oak woodwork in both the furniture and architraves, which mark the subtle changes from single to double interior height. The sweep of a room is often primarily vertical, so that banding along the walls is used as a type of horizontal channel that directs attention along the main axis of interior spaces. Wright designed over 100 individual examples of furniture for the house.

# WARD W. WILLITS RESIDENCE

Constructed: 1902
Address: 1445 Sheridan Road, Highland Park, Illinois

This has been called Wright's first house in pure Prairie Style. It took advantage of a spacious suburban site upon which Wright could begin to stretch out the wings and profile of this domestic building type. The landscaping was designed concurrently with the building; a process which Wright believed was important in achieving a complete unity of design. Inside, the main living spaces revolve around the domestic focal point of the hearth, as in virtually all of Wright's Prairie Style homes. The exterior is composed of a series of vertical and horizontal interlocking planes and masses, and there is a constant interplay between solidity, transparency, and open spaces both piercing and surrounding the building. This is especially noticeable along the primary axis of the house. It is established by the long horizontal line that begins at one end in the open, roofed veranda, then runs through the house and terminates with the *porte-cochere* (a porch without a balustrade which could accommodate wheeled vehicles) at the opposite end. Two of the most important rooms of the house open directly to the landscape. The living room, with its floor-to-ceiling windows opens onto an exclusive low-walled terrace with cement planters, and the dining room has access to the covered terrace.

Domestic ritual was an important aspect in all of Wright's designs. During this period, Wright's clientele was largely comprised of the well-to-do, who had considerable means at their disposal, and whose

RIGHT: Dark wood trim encases and enlivens the stucco surfaces of this Prairie house, and was one of the hallmarks of Wright's individual Prairie Style. The trim is used to formally define and strengthen the impact of the flat geometric divisions of the walls, but it is also one of the key elements in Wright's architectural composition. It acts as a sort of wooden "screen," which develops a surface rhythm across the wings of the house. Wright called this rhythm the "eye-mosaic," which gave interest and variety to an otherwise modest stucco surface.

LEFT: The *porte-cochere*, shown in the upper right corner of this image, is the shorter of the two rectangles which make up the long, central axis running through the building. The mass of the house is set just off-center along that axis, while the formal, open parapet situated at the front of the building—outside the living room— is also off-set just to one side. This subtle and highly refined adjustment of form by Wright is one of the factors that lend his designs such sophisticated intricacy.

lifestyle greatly influenced Wright's designs for their homes. From the *porte-cochere*, the house was entered through the comparatively compressed and formal reception area, a symbolic space in which guests removed and stored their street clothing and prepared to be welcomed into the private domain of the home. From that compressed space, the substantial living and dining rooms opened up beyond the main stair upon entering the core of the house. As a result, the visitor encountered a series of symbolic and real spaces, which structurally alternated between expansion and contraction—ritual and welcome.

RIGHT, ABOVE: A vertical repeat is created along the frontage of the house by the application of dark wood trim between the lateral "piers" of the facade. The trim serves to outline and divide the exterior, individual panels of the living room's floor-to-ceiling windows. It then continues upward over the stucco plane of the mid-facade to form the five windows of the second floor. The vertical pattern of the trim runs directly upward from the base to be topped by the underside of the protruding eaves.

RIGHT, BELOW: Behind the Willits house stands a gardener's cottage with stables. The original wood and plaster structure, with a design in keeping with the Prarie Style, has since been remodeled.

# EDWIN H. CHENEY HOUSE

Constructed: 1903
Address: 520 North East Avenue, Oak Park, Illinois. Tel: 708-524-2067
The house remains in private hands and there are no tours. However, it is
    currently operated as a bed-and-breakfast establishment for which reservations
    are required.

The primary floor is elevated approximately 5ft. (1.5m) above ground level enhancing its isolation from surrounding suburban activity and adding to its character as a refuge. The design nevertheless retains its earth-hugging character, not least because the basement itself is recessed into the earth and only detectable from the back and rear sides of the house.

The front door is reached by a private walk to the far right side of the property, so that the terrace is reached only by first penetrating the private domain of the house and then exiting from the leaded French doors of the living room. The terrace functions as a private and protected part of the landscape, removed from the world at large. This is the very first instance in which Wright separated a frontal exterior terrace from the entry path to the house, and this design became a major motif in all of his most important later Prairie houses. Inside, the front of the house is comprised a single vista from the dining room at the north end, through the living room in the center, and into the library at the south. Different functional areas are not divided by

RIGHT: The dining room occupies the north end of the axis of "public" areas, which comprise the length of the frontal interior. The leaded art glass windows reinforce the sense of refuge of the house. Their screening quality immediately imparts the feeling of being hidden from view, and are a design solution that allows natural light on the one hand, and privacy on the other. They symbolise Wright's definition of the domestic residence as the site of safety and security.

RIGHT: Originally the front exterior of the property was enclosed by high masonry parapet walls, enhancing the acute sense of seclusion Wright instilled in this particular design. The Cheney house was by necessity located very close to the sidewalk at the front of the property. The brick parapet was stretched across the full frontal width of the site, restricting views into the site from both frontal and diagonal lines of sight, and solving what to Wright was the incessant problem of privacy.

INSET: The massive low-lying masonry block of the house is bound at the center of a maze of brick parapet walls. At their center is a raised terrace hidden behind a high brick wall, which comes forward from the house and is accessible only through the living room. Although the terrace in many ways functions as a traditional American front porch might in providing a vertical and lateral prospect open to the sky, in this case it is unique for being an entirely enclosed portion of the ramparts of the house, and for not being part of any path of entry to the front door.

ABOVE: The main interior spaces of the house are raised above street level, and sit above a basement floor—unusual in Wright's Prairie houses—which was at one time the residence of Mrs. Cheney's sister. The house is small, square in plan and its form condensed into closely compact volumes, both on the exterior and interior. The main floor has leaded casement windows, although the basement has the more traditional American sash window type located in the center of the sides of the lower facade. conventional walls, but rather by intervening vertical and horizontal features, which define the sub-divisions of the spaces. In the living room the hearth has been recessed rather deeply beneath the low-hung ceiling, and is bracketed by walls of book shelves on both sides. Opposite the fireplace are the leaded-glass, French-style doors leading to the private terrace overlooking the street at the front of the house.

ABOVE: The interior of the house is punctuated by the substantial masonry mass of the fireplace. Behind it there is an extended gallery that marks the lateral axis of the building. Bedrooms as private spaces are situated off the gallery along the rear of the house, while the front length is given over to the zoned or open-plan living areas, which mark the more public domain. The living room is situated at the center. Its rich interior and low-hung beamed ceiling are characterized by the extensive use of dark red-stained fir trim.

# HIRAM BALDWIN HOUSE

Constructed: 1905
Address: 205 Essex Road, Kenilworth, Illinois

A more compact type of Prairie house, the Hiram Baldwin residence reiterates the dominant theme of this style with an exterior combining cement stucco and dark-stained wood trim. In this case the upper facades have been completely darkened, and their recessed position set in gentle contrast to the lighter undersides of the overhanging eaves. These sections of the house seem to recede indefinitely inward towards the core, and from some views of the house are hardly visible at all, giving an overwhelming impression of privacy and seclusion. Clearly a suburban dwelling, the house is of a more modest scale than many others by Wright. But the natural beauty of its materials blend effortlessly with the trees and foliage of its large corner site. The house and landscaping quietly accentuate one another.

The house has typical Prairie features. Wright believed ideally that a house should be set up, off the ground in order to provide a better view of the surrounding prairie. In the Baldwin house he eliminated any basement, and replaced it with a stylobate that acted like a pedestal beneath the house. Walls rise immediately from that base up to the roof, and the second story facade demonstrates a continuous band of casement windows beneath the roof. The development of Wright's style grew with each house he designed, and the early Prairie residences provided the prototype for the later, and perhaps more modest, ones such as this.

RIGHT: Outside the front door, Wright has inserted another, but smaller, more subdued and less robust, transitional space that must be traversed in order to gain access to the house. By using this device, he insists on an indirect approach to the interior. A visitor is sheltered beneath a roof and enclosed by walls on three of four sides, but remains outside the door.

FOLLOWING PAGES: The building's low proportions and gently sloping roof give a sheltering impression. Upper floors extend beyond the mass of the lower level, but are themselves nestled beneath the overhang of the eaves, producing an upward and outward movement to some sides of the elevation.

LEFT: Wright greatly preferred the use of open-swinging casement windows in all his Prairie houses. For each project the window proportions were individually determined, and each sash could be tailored to receive leaded glass if Wright chose. Smooth sand-finished stucco was used as the final rendering of the exterior. The appearance of the surface might change depending on how its porous texture deepens in hue with shadow from direct or indirect sunlight. Wright often broke conventional engineering practice by the depth of cantilevering of his roofs. This could be achieved by stiffening rods running from the cantilever into the top of the house and through to the masonry mass of the fireplace and chimney.

LEFT: In *An Autobiography*, Wright observed that "a little height on the prairie was enough to look like much more—every detail as to height becoming intensely significant." Although not especially tall, upper reaches of the house seem to hover among the trees from some perspectives. The great depth of the under-eaves is a remarkably straightforward design solution to roofing both the building and the upper terrace at the same time. But it is more intoxicating than its mere function allows, for its horizontal plane impresses as though it were part of the vast expanse of the prairie sky. It is compressive and expansive at the same time.

ABOVE: The interior of the house has been remodeled, but many of the original features remain. The door slab is composed of vertical and horizontal slabs inset with leaded panels of translucent glass. In many of Wright's Prairie houses the pattern would be carried over from the more ornate window panels, but remain composed of strips or even squares. The house does not have a centrally placed front door, as is typical of the Prairie Style's predilection for asymmetry. As the entryway is offset from the main rooms of the house, a visitor enters into a spatially constricted waiting area, and is at the same time in the interior, yet outside of the home.

# W. R. HEATH HOUSE

Constructed: 1905
Address: 76 Soldiers Place, Buffalo, New York

A brick Prairie house with an imposing sense of structural mass, the Heath residence is nevertheless a graceful play of layered forms and hidden volumes, which from some angles can only be glimpsed as the house recedes into the distance. The house is married to the ground by its gently sloping roof line, yet maintains a formidable impression. Typically, color is reduced to the natural shades of the materials. The exterior of the house is typical of Wright's deep veneration for the rolling Midwestern countryside. The classic motifs of the Wrightian Prairie house—the low-hung gabled roofs, the distended eaves, and the stretches of encircling walls—are symbolic of the prairie itself, and combine to overcome the limited real space of the suburban lot.

Viewed from some, but not all sides, it is clear that Wright interjected an intentional asymmetry as a personal expression of his artistic intentions. The house boasts a large covered porch as part of the T-shaped ground plan. Its forms are staggered, giving variety and repose to both the external and internal aspects. It has been noted that although Wright's first journey to Japan occurred during the year the house was built, there is little if any influence of a Japanese aesthetic evident here.

RIGHT: The original leaded glass windows for the house were designed so that the decorative motif—unlike that in many other Prairie houses—was not complete within the borders of every sash, but was instead carried horizontally across the whole of the facade through the evenly set rows of windows, forming a continuous band of patterned art glass running through each casement window. Wright often accentuated the part played by fenestration in every composition, preferring to align his windows in ribbon-like bands across the surfaces of each facade.

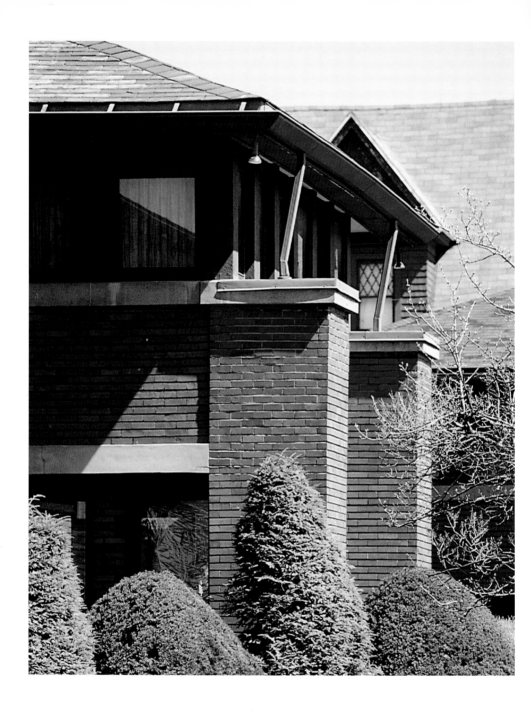

ABOVE: Wright often played with the relationship between vertical and horizontal features, accentuating cubic volumes by bringing part of the facade forward on hefty vertical piers. His passion for detailing as an integral part of any building was reflected in the continuation of this vertical and horizontal play even within the laying of flat, dark red Roman bricks, as seen in many of the Prairie houses. Horizontal mortar joints are recessed into the grooves of traditional pointing, but the vertical mortar joint was rendered flush with the surface of the brick wall.

ABOVE: The exteriors of Wright's Prairie houses took their inspiration from his deep veneration for the rolling Midwestern countryside. Low parapets often incorporated troughs or depressions for vegetation, and acted as bases for massive cement bowls, which carried plantings reminiscent of prairie life.

LEFT: From early on, Wright showed a keen awareness of the comparative properties of his construction materials. He argued against fashions that sought to disguise the true properties of natural materials such as stone, wood, and different types of brick by painting over them or adding stucco. Throughout his career he was careful to reveal the true state of all materials, and to incorporate a variety of natural surface textures as important design factors in his buildings. Brick, for example, which he used frequently during the Prairie house phase, was first a product of the earth and only then a product of the kiln. When amassed in the form of great piers across a facade, it gave a rich glowing effect of earth-toned hues which could not be reproduced by other materials.

# FREDERICK C. ROBIE HOUSE

Constructed: 1906–08
Address: 5757 South Woodlawn Avenue,Chicago, Illinois. Tel: 773-702-2150
Owned by the University of Chicago, the house has been designated a National
   Historic Landmark by the American Institute of Architects. Restoration has
   been undertaken by the Frank Lloyd Wright Home and Studio Foundation.
   Guided tours are available Monday through Friday at 11am, 1pm and 3pm,
   and on Saturday and Sunday from 11am to 3pm.

Generally considered the most accomplished example of Wright's Prairie Style, the Robie house has nonetheless been criticized by some scholars for the severity and inconsistencies in Wright's design of its interior spaces. The patron, Frederick Robie was a bicycle manufacturer and engineer, whose search for an architect sympathetic to his own passion for modern construction forms and materials led him to Wright.

The exterior of the house is a formidable low-lying mass constructed of flat Roman brick masonry that is narrower than usual, steel, and concrete. Its three striking horizontal strata are a summary of the Prairie School aesthetic that favors long, earth-bound dwellings. The 20ft. (6m) cantilevered eaves that appear to hover above the terraces are among the most dramatic and elongated in Wright's *oeuvre*. They are held in place by protracted steel beams, and remain something of an engineering phenomenon, particularly within the context of a domestic residence.

The individual rows of brick were flush mortared along the vertical joints, but raked into recesses along the horizontal joints—a fine detail of construction, which subtly emphasized the predominant horizontal

RIGHT: The Milwaukee firm of Niedecken–Walbridge, who had worked with Wright since 1904, realized Wright's designs for the interior of Robie house. Much of the furniture from the house survives and a majority of the leaded glass remains in situ. The design of the art glass was based on the abstraction of two flowers set to each side of an angular, geometric composition, echoing the actual floor plan of the house.

line of the house. In this case, the house does not rest upon a basement. Wright deftly substituted a concrete stylobate, or watertable, to serve the same purpose. The three dominant horizontal tiers of the house are graded from the longest and lowest nearest the ground, to the most narrow and deeply set at the top. They are asymmetrically positioned, and were constructed upon a skeleton of steel beams and brick piers.

The architectural philosophy of the prarie is emphatic within the character of the house. Bedrooms are located on the third floor, with a billiard room, children's playroom, and an adjoining three-car garage annex on the first floor level. The second floor was entirely given over to the main living and dining areas. Together they form a single, uninterrupted long and low interior space punctuated in the center by the brick fireplace and central stair. A running band of wide windows across the front length of the room, and an open corridor positioned axially along each side of the huge hearth effectively rejoin the two living spaces into one. At the far end of both the living and dining areas there is a triangular-shaped bay that juts outward,

LEFT: The site that the house was built on was much smaller, did not have an extensive garden, and was more restricted than Wright had usually encountered. Landscaping was problematic because the garden, as such, lies immediately along the street in view of all who pass. The genius of the house can be recognized in Wright's cunning use of angles, recesses, lines, and projections to overcome any feeling of "closed" or static surfaces.

ABOVE: In order to offset the impenetrable mass of the house against the softer effects of nature, Wright distributed low-roofed porches, terraces and "hanging" balconies from as many levels as possible. Not all of the visible parapet walls adjoin real balconies, but only indicate "holes" or spatial volumes in the composition, which are used to carry forward the dominant horizontal of the house. Wright also raised cement planters dramatically above the ground line so that their sculptural forms and foliage plantings would become a prominent part of the view looking out from the interior.

ABOVE: There is an "enclosing" and ritualistic quality to much of Wright's furniture design from the Prairie period. Like some of the other more elaborate Prairie houses, Wright designed an encompassing decorative program for the Robie house.

RIGHT: The centrally located fireplace provides the only separation between living and dining rooms that form a single, uninterrupted long and low interior space. A row of wide windows and corridors run along either side of the hearth to combine the rooms into one.

interrupting the otherwise strict rectangles of the elevation. These unusual features have often been referred to as the "prow" of a ship. Wright's designs for the house also included textiles, light fixtures and fittings, leaded art glass, and furnishings.

Much of the furniture from the house survives and is conserved at the University of Chicago's David and Alfred Smart Gallery. The majority of the leaded art glass also survives in situ. Their design was formed around the abstraction of two flowers set to each side of an angular, geometric composition, which is based on the actual floor plan of the house.

# MEYER MAY HOUSE

Constructed: 1908
Address: 450 Madison Avenue, Southeast, Grand Rapids, Michigan.
 Tel: 616-246-4821
Free tours are available on Tuesdays and Thursdays from 10am to 2pm, and on
 Sundays from 1-5pm.

Although he often expressed his intentions in designing a type of domestic home that was supremely appropriate to the landscape of the Midwestern prairie, the term "Prairie house" was not used by Wright himself. However, the name has come to represent the residential dwellings he designed between approximately 1900 and 1911. Like other Prairie School architects practicing in Chicago during the earliest years of the twentieth century, Wright formulated a style of house that reflected the most unique and beautiful qualities of a landscape he so admired.

The May house is deceptively small, and its plan remarkably compact. As in most, but not all, of Wright's Prairie designs, the underside of the eaves has been painted in a lighter hue, serving to accentuate their depth and quality as a continuous band, while also reflecting natural light into darker interior rooms. His design philosophy dictated that architectural simplicity and restfulness required consistency of materials. Therefore his Prairie houses were either primarily brick or stucco overall, both materials appropriate for the addition of wood trim. In the few instances where Wright did combine materials, especially on the exterior elevation, the application of those materials was separated by the main features of the elevation, so that each story gained a unique but coordinated identity. The interior of the May house was executed by the Niedecken-Walbridge company who collaborated on many other Wright houses. The house has been carefully restored.

RIGHT: The intricate colored art glass of this house is among the most well-known of Wright's leaded glass designs. Typically, the motifs were conventionalized and abstracted from plant forms found in nature, and are representative of regional prairie vegetation. The ribbon of windows running horizontally across the ground floor facade is interrupted by a rhythm of slender brick piers. These enhance the windows that are set back from the surface of the facade, and the play of varying surface levels on the exterior.

ABOVE: The May house is an outstanding example of Wright's designs in its height and proportions, which reflect the quiet horizon. The house was positioned at the far end of the site in order to allow for as much landscaping as possible and to firmly establish the line of the house against the line of the horizon. Although the second-story terrace and the lateral porch were subsequently enclosed, the asymmetrical off-setting of the roofline continues to make the exterior elevation one of the most engaging in Wright's Prairie designs.

# GEORGE STOCKMAN HOUSE

Constructed: 1908

Address: 530 First Street, North East, Mason City, Iowa.

Tel: 515-421-3666/423-1923

Tours are available June to August, Thursday through Saturday from 10am to 5pm, and on Sunday from 1–5pm; from September through October only on Saturday and Sunday.

The house was moved from its original location in 1989 to the present site, and was purchased by the River City Society for historic preservation. It is unique in that it was the only domestic design by Wright to be constructed in Mason City, Iowa. However it was typical of his prescription for how families and individuals in a democracy should organize their relationship to the outside world. Brendan Gill's biography of Wright (1987) observed that "If the Prairie House had little to do with an actual prairie, it had a great deal to do with how Wright believed people should live. . ." The Stockman house, as with other Prarie houses, erects barriers against the outside while diminishing the usual compartmentalization of the rooms within.

Consistent with the intricacies of Wright's level of patronage, the commission came from Dr. George Stockman, whose friends, James Blythe and J. Markley, had already commissioned two structures from Wright in the same Midwestern city—the Park Inn Hotel and the City National Bank. The house is virtually square in form, with the entryway on one side and a covered terrace on the opposite side providing a short lateral axis. Bedrooms are situated on the upper floor, and following convention the kitchen is sited at the rear. The living and dining rooms spread over the ground floor as one large uninterrupted space with only the hearth positioned between.

RIGHT: The in-built furnishings of a Prairie house diminished the client's need to "import" their own taste. Cupboards, sideboards, shelves, and screens of both wooden slats and glass—with their continuous wood banding, their emphatic geometry, and their intersecting planes and shapes—were typically designed by Wright to reflect the architectural character of the exterior of the house. Glass-fronted bookcases were frequently used by Wright as another display of banded, leaded, or stained art glass.

LEFT: Typical of a Wrightian Prairie house, the windows are distributed evenly in horizontal bands across the facade, serving to define from the exterior the varying levels of interior living space. Continuous running wood trim both delineates and wraps the corners of the main block-like form of the house, and continues as a visually prominent element along the border of the extending eaves, the base of the house, and the darkened window frames. The trim serves both to define and unite the design of the house as an overall geometric composition.

BELOW: Not only in principle, but in construction, the Prairie house erected barriers against the outside while diminishing the usual "box" arrangement of the rooms within. For Wright, families were dynamic units sharing their domestic activities, as well as having a fundamental need for privacy from the outside world.

ABOVE: Inside the Stockman house, the Prairie ideal of interior family space was personified by the placement of the massive hearth at the center of the home. Around it, there is unbroken access from one open-plan area, such as the dining room or library, to another, but the brick chimney continued to define the identity of the living room as a place of warmth and comfort. The low-hung ceilings also reinforced the feeling of enclosure and offered Wright the opportunity to continually experiment with different forms and heights of interior lighting.

RIGHT: Despite the generally urban or suburban siting of Wright's Prairie houses, he never lost sight of the human need for plantings, either in the form of extensive landscaping, or the more modest presence of raised beds before the windows. Gardens signified harmony with the local landscape, and were individualized in design and form for each site.

# HENRY J. ALLEN HOUSE

Constructed: 1917
Address: 255 North Roosevelt Avenue, Wichita, Kansas, Tel: 316-687-1027
Guided tours are available if booked at least ten days in advance.

The house was commissioned from Wright by Elsie Allen as a residence for herself and her husband, at one time a United States senator, state governor, and publisher. The Allens lived in the house until 1949. The property has since been sympathetically restored, and was purchased by the Allen-Lambe Foundation. It is Wright's only domestic design to be built in Kansas. The exterior appears to be of brick Prairie Style, and is among the last of his mature expressions of that type of building. It is of an L-shaped plan with a one-story wing extending toward the front of the property containing a massive living room, adjoined only by the entryway. Behind, the house rises to two levels, with the dining room, kitchen, and staff areas below, and the bedrooms, guest rooms, a library, and a private study above.

During the time Wright was designing the house he was also formulating his ideas for the Imperial Hotel in Tokyo. Although he had first visited Japan in 1905, he did not contribute to the architectural character of the country until he began to design the hotel in 1915. Construction began in 1917, the same year as the Allen house, and the influence of the one upon the other is apparent. The Allen house's enclosed garden courtyard includes a pond, and a Japanese-style "teahouse." In this way the house departs from Wright's earlier Prairie house formula, although the influence of Japan had been subtly evident in his work for some time.

RIGHT:  In an interesting revelation about the aesthetic relationship between Wright and his clients, David Hanks has pointed out that although Allen clearly appreciated Wright's unusual designs for the house's walnut furnishings, he subsequently went straight to Niedecken requesting more comfortable, revival-style Jacobean furniture for his home. Professionally, Wright and Niedecken shared similar aesthetic values, and Niedecken was one of the first American interior designers to argue in print for a closer collaboration between an architect and a "decorator" of interiors.

LEFT: The dramatic horizontal disposition of the house is exemplary of Wright's Prairie house style, and attests to the pedigree of the Allen house as among his later Prairie designs. As a statement of his principles of suburban domestic architecture, the facade is devoid of traditional decorative or individualizing features. Rather, the temper of the building is set by the easy spatial flow between the surrounding grounds and the galleries beneath the *porte-cochere* and the eaves. Around a Prairie house, Wright configured a series of terraces, balconies, and sheltered porches, which by providing private access to nature were invaluable for outdoor living on comparatively constricted suburban lots.

ABOVE: The Milwaukee firm of Niedecken–Walbridge, who had begun cooperation with Wright in 1904, and advertised themselves as "Specialists in design and execution of Interior Decorations and Mural Paintings, Makers of Special Furniture—Art Glass—Electric Fixtures," supervised the execution of the interiors of the Allen house. They were also involved with many other interiors by Wright, including that of the famous Robie house in Chicago. In the case of the Allen house, Wright specified his designs for furniture in studio drawings, then passed these to Niedecken for realization.

RIGHT: The interior of the Allen house was uncommonly elegant with its living room of nearly 1,000sq. ft. (93sq. m) and gabled ceilings inset with parallel rows of lamps framed beneath ornamental grills. Wright included the use of leaded art glass both in the windows, and for the glazing of furniture doors. He also had the horizontal masonry joints, or interior "pointing," covered with gold leaf to echo the richness of the interior decorative scheme.

# HERBERT F. JOHNSON HOUSE, "WINGSPREAD"

Constructed: 1937

Address: 33 East Four Mile Road, Wind Point, Wisconsin

The property was restored in 1977, and is presently a conference centre. It is recommended that visitors contact the centre to arrange mutually convenient hours, as the building is not always open to the public. The Johnson Foundation, PO Box 547, Racine, Wisconsin. Tel: 414-639-3353

The house is sometimes referred to as "Wingspread," and was commissioned by Herbert Johnson, who had also commissioned the Johnson Wax building in Racine, Wisconsin, of 1936. Despite its date, Wright himself said that "Wingspread" was the last of his Prairie houses.

The central core of the complex is an imposing and abstract three-story octagon. From it, the pinwheel plan of the building spreads forth. In this instance however, the four separate wings of the house are in part laid alongside the octagon, increasing its volume and serving as a secondary base from which the central upper floors arise. The interior living space, called the Great Hall, rises in three floors at the centre of the building. Open plan areas for different activities are distributed throughout those floors. There is a dining area, built-in benches in the living spaces, three desk areas, and a mezzanine. On three sides of each floor of the Great Hall are two-story doors. The house is a fine example of how Wright planned every structure to work in unison with its particular site.

RIGHT: Interior spaces in "Wingspread" are on a variety of levels, creating clear divisions of space between the library, living, and dining areas of the Great Hall. The mezzanine level functions as an internal parapet facilitating movement through the house, but also providing intimate viewing and seating areas, as can be seen here.

RIGHT: The pinnacle of the house provides dramatic views over the site. Before the house was completed and landscaped, the site was a flat stretch of prairie characterized by a pond and meandering ravine. Wright designed and sited "Wingspread" to take the best possible advantage of these natural features.

BELOW: The wings of the house were "zoned" or distinguished by their individual functions. One wing was reserved for guests; another for utility, cooking areas, and staff quarters; and a third for the Johnsons' children. Each of these wings was single-story, on the same low-lying level. The fourth or "Master" wing was built over two levels, and storage was on the ground floor. Above this there is a substantial terrace belonging to the "Master" wing, in addition to a cantilevered wooden balcony that dramatically emerges 'from the supporting brickwork, and appears to hover above the lawn. It is crowned by a wooden canopy.

ABOVE: Not unlike Wright's earlier "classic" Prairie Houses, at "Wingspread" the structure seems to naturally follow the topography of the site and the line of the horizon so that it is sometimes difficult to tell where the land ends and the building begins. The house does indeed appear to effortlessly "spread" over the site, while the ravine at its east border seems to originate with the house as much as with nature itself.

LEFT: The central brick fireplace core, which runs up through the living spaces of the building in the shape of a massive column, has five separate fireplaces and five flues set into it. A spiral stair rises alongside giving immediate access to all floors. Surrounding the great chimney are three vertical bands of continuous clerestory windows.

ABOVE: Wright said that "Wingspread" was his best-built and among his most expensive houses. Materials were often specialized. For the swimming pool he employed pink Kasota sand, enriching the natural hues of the complex overall. Seen in profile, it is clear that the house took as its precedent the pinwheel form of the earlier William Martin house, but greatly enlarged upon that prototype by amassing the central core over three floors, extending the elevation of the plan substantially.

RIGHT: Wright wrote about "Wingspread" in An Autobiography, remarking on the high caliber of the workmanship, particularly in the laying of the masonry. Through his choice of materials, Wright proved his ability to successfully combine the natural properties, textures, and colors of diverse elements into a unique architectural composition.

# GAZETTEER

---

## FRANK WRIGHT THOMAS HOUSE, "THE HAREM"

**Constructed:** 1901
**Address:** 210 Forest Avenue, Oak Park, Illinois
The house is included in the Walking Tours of Wright Houses in Oak Park sponsored by the Frank Lloyd Wright Home and Studio Foundation, 951 Chicago Avenue, Oak Park, Illinois. Tel: 708-848-1976

The earliest of Wright's Oak Park Prairie Style homes, the house was originally commissioned by James C. Rogers, but was presented to Mr. and Mrs. Frank Wright Thomas, his daughter and son-in-law, when construction was finished. Storrer pointed out that for many years the building was inappropriately shingle surfaced, and was restored to its original plaster rendering only from 1975 onward. The house has a typical Prairie, asymmetrical L-plan, the shorter wing formed on the street side of the property by the considerable "breakfront," which moves outward from the long mass of the building. Inside, the house boasts Wright's first gabled ceiling dining area.

LEFT: The length of the house is emphasized by the rows of contrasting horizontal banding. Between these bands, narrower ribbons of art glass windows create a balance of varying surface textures, and give the house an overall bejewelled appearance. The strongly architectural motif of the rounded arch placed at the entryway is typical of early Prairie house design, appearing with equal prominence at, for example, the Dana and the Heurtley houses, both built in 1902.

# CHARLES S. ROSS HOUSE

**Constructed:** 1902
**Address:** 3211 South Shore Drive, Lake Delavan, Wisconsin

Now an extensive and spacious cottage, the Ross house was originally a T-plan Prairie structure, subsequently modified to become cruciform in shape. The facing is typically made from board-and-batten. Storrer pointed out that the building's initial dark-stained surface was later overpainted, the veranda enclosed, and the second floor also enlarged. Darker banding against the lighter painted surfaces, however, clearly continues to delineate the typical Wrightian horizontality of the structure, while the division of exterior surfaces into distinct horizontal zones effectively binds the house to the landscape in characteristic Prairie Style.

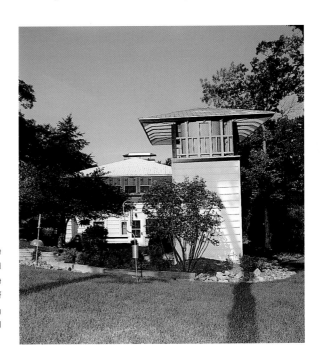

RIGHT: The influence of Japanese design upon Wright is already perceptible in this building in its subdued decorative detailing, its dramatic abstract play of light against dark geometric shape, and the feeling of lightness that comes from the depth of the protruding eaves. Wright's keen sense of the purity of architectural form is present throughout.

# GEORGE AND DELTA BARTON HOUSE

**Constructed:** 1903
**Address:** 118 Summit Avenue, Buffalo, New York. Tel: 716-856-3858
Tours by reservation; Saturday 10am, Sunday 1pm.

Originally belonging to the Darwin Martin house "complex," the Barton residence was the first of many houses designed by Wright for executives and employees of the Larkin Company. The house was commissioned by Martin for his sister and brother-in-law, and was constructed on a substantial corner site, which later also included Martin's magnificent, but larger residence. The two houses shared an adjoining garage and a greenhouse. The Barton house is of cruciform plan with each primary living space situated in each of the four wings: the dining room in the west wing; living rooms in the east; the kitchen comprising the north wing; and the entryway and open verandas placed in the southern wing. This internal distribution of living space is reflected in the exterior of the building, and is characteristic of the clarity with which Wright's domestic designs responded to the requirements of contemporary living.

LEFT: Another of the somewhat fortress-like Prairie houses, the Barton residence emphasizes the placement of inset casement windows—a form Wright greatly preferred—the sheltering quality of the low-hipped roof, and the horizontal courses of textured masonry left in a natural state.

# MARY M. W. ADAMS HOUSE

**Constructed:** 1905
**Address:** 1923 Lake Avenue, Highland Park, Illinois

Sited on a corner lot, the house necessarily presents two main views from the exterior. One of these displays the gabled "breakfront" of the first story, while on the other there is a two-story rectangular form, which is forward from the main facade. Located near Lake Michigan, the building has a wooden frame, Prairie structure. Both its form and the details of the exterior are delineated once again through an abstract patterning of light and dark horizontal bands. These emphasize how the different architectural forms are situated forward and back in the overall composition, and also serve to ground the building to the site.

ABOVE: A plaster-surfaced Prairie residence, the Adams house is a thoroughly organic approach to domestic architectural design. Its welcoming arms move out naturally from the main mass of the building, yet it retains the feeling of a private, protective enclosure, which is particularly relevant in the light of its corner position.

# WILLIAM. A. GLASNER HOUSE

**Constructed:** 1905
**Address:** 850 Sheridan Road, Glencoe, Illinois

Remodeled on two separate occasions and subsequently restored in the early 1970s, the Glasner house is unusual in its plan, which refuses to conform to any of Wright's standard Prairie types. This is except for the interior spaces that circulate outward from a single axis, in this case running east to west. Some features of the original plan were never executed, and it is difficult to classify the building as a typically Wrightian Prairie home despite its date. However, as Storrer acknowledged, notable features include an interior organization of space, which prefigures Wright's later Usonian type in the absence of a distinct dining area. The house is also of interest to connoisseurs of Wright's work because it incorporates glass panes that become iridescent on whichever single side receives the most light at a given time.

LEFT: Rough hewn timber was consistently specified by Wright for the board-and-batten surfacing of a Prairie house facade. This building, unlike other examples of Wright's Prairie houses, was properly and sympathetically remodeled and later restored using the correct materials, which were originally selected by Wright not for financial, but for aesthetic and ideological reasons.

# A. W. GRIDLEY HOUSE

**Constructed:** 1906
**Address:** 605 North Batavia Avenue, Batavia, Illinois

An excellent example of how architecturally refined the Prairie Style could be in Wright's hands, the Gridley house has a typical cruciform plan. The first floor rises upon the narrow stylobate in a cruciform plan, while the casement windows on this floor are merely given a narrow banding at their base, which does not exceed the width of the window. Otherwise the first floor walls are plainly rendered until the centrally positioned "breakfront" merges easily into the open porch. The second floor is of an abbreviated T-plan, and appears deceptively narrower along the exterior, immediately beneath the outward thrust of the eaves.

ABOVE: The long and low open porch forms the dramatic base of the building's T-plan. Its stucco-rendered protective walls recall those of higher elevation at the Pettit Memorial Chapel, but here their lower, open format provides an important 180-degree view over the slightly rising hill of the site.

# D. P. HOYT HOUSE

**Constructed:** 1906
**Address:** 318 South Fifth, Geneva, Illinois

This square-plan Prairie house has an exterior delineated by characteristic dark-stained wood trim set against plaster rendering. The box-like structure is considerably lightened by the geometric wood trim running in three horizontal layers across the facades, and ending in vertical bands at the corners. The leading of the casement windows partially repeats the patterning of the facade, creating the impression of an overall screen of vertical and horizontal lines. The whole is anchored by the broad overhang of the eaves, another consistent Wrightian motif, which is here repeated in the simple hipped roof of the entrance.

LEFT: The combination of dark-stained wood trim highlighted against the plastered surfaces of the walls can give a particularly Oriental impression, not least because of Wright's use of the screen motif, which ties strong horizontal elements into more delicate vertical ones. The linear patterning of Wright's Prairie Style is often much less apparent on the exterior, while on the interior of his Prairie Style buildings it can govern the subtle, overall decorative composition.

# GEORGE MADISON MILLARD HOUSE

**Constructed:** 1906
**Address:** 1689 Lake Avenue, Highland Park, Illinois

In its cruciform, first floor plan this house is not unlike the Gridley House in Batavia, but here the "breakfront" shows a partially open porch on the second floor, which is also in a T-plan format. A long open porch extends away from the center of the house on the ground floor, again offering a much desired access to the landscape, while simultaneously providing shelter. The board-and-batten facing here produces a very different overall effect from the light stucco rendering of the Gridley house, despite the close similarity in plan, while the rows of windows extend around the whole of the facade.

ABOVE: The house was built in a forested site into which the Prairie Style seemed a natural addition. Wright provided George Millard with a sympathetic home, whose materials clearly reflected the environment of surrounding woodland, and which lay low and close to the ground within the trees.

# W. H. PETTIT MEMORIAL CHAPEL

**Constructed:** 1906
**Address:** Harrison at Webster, Belvidere, Illinois. Tel: 815-547-7642
The Chapel can be visited from 8am–12 noon, 1–4 pm, Mondays to Fridays.

The wood and stucco chapel borders the Belvidere cemetery. It is a diminutive and very modest structure to which the horizontal disposition and low-hung, sheltered qualities of the Prairie Style are supremely appropriate. Each wing of the chapel terminates in a protective porch, which increases functional space, while also providing sheltered reception areas. The chapel was commissioned from Wright by Emma Glasner Pettit in memory of her husband who had spent his youth in Belvidere. Restoration was begun in the early 1980s based on surviving drawings and photographs.

LEFT: Rising from a cement stylobate, the high plaster-surfaced bearing walls lend privacy to the interior. This scheme also eliminated unwanted noise from the outside, while the ribbon windows comprised of art glass allowed sufficient, but diffuse light.

RIGHT: The pitched ceiling of the interior reflects the low, hipped roof of the Prairie Style design. The banding of horizontal wood trim on the exterior is repeated on the inside of the chapel. Characteristically, a brick hearth is centralized in the plan, and is surrounded by simple spindle-backed wooden folding chairs.

# AVERY COONLEY HOUSE

**Constructed:** 1907
**Address:** 300 Scottswood Road, Riverside, Illinois

The house is a fine example of Wright's philosophy that the design process for a residential project was an ongoing one. Hanks has pointed out that Wright often returned to properties to make architectural and interior additions or alterations, and that the Coonley family continued to supplement their Wright-designed furnishings with further ones commissioned from the architect for many years after the house was complete. The interiors of the Coonley house were supervised and executed for Wright by the Milwaukee firm of Niedecken–Walbridge, who were also closely involved with the realization of the Robie house interiors. In Wright's own opinion, the Coonley house was the best of all his Prairie residences, and one in which he was given complete freedom by his patrons to actualize a completely integrated Prairie design tailored to the precise and intimate requirements of the future occupants.

ABOVE: Designs for the Avery Coonley house were executed and exhibited during 1907, and construction commenced in the following year. The stark horizontal lines of its essentially U-shaped plan appear to emerge from the ground beneath, so that the rambling building is seen to become part of the existing site.

LEFT: The house was given rich decorative effects throughout. Texture and color were applied to exterior surfaces by, for example, the use of polychrome tiles with conventionalized tulip motifs. Wright's initial use of this spectacular decorative device was in the Coonley house.

## STEPHEN M. B. HUNT HOUSE (I)

**Constructed:** 1907
**Address:** 345 South Seventh Avenue, La Grange, Illinois

Storrer and other sources point out that this is the first and best residence to be constructed according to Wright's designs for "A Fireproof House of $5000," which he published in *The Ladies' Home Journal* in 1901. Although the original plans specified building in fireproof concrete, in the end the house was constructed of wood with plaster rendering. The building is cruciform in plan, the lateral porch—now enclosed—providing sculptural relief from the severity of the massive block of the house.

ABOVE: Again, the facade is treated as an abstract composition in contrasting vertical and horizontal lines and planes, and the eaves jut outward from the former porch to shelter the drive. Casement windows are bordered by broad, dark bands of wood trim, emphasizing their importance for both the decorative and functional aspects of the overall design.

# ALEXANDER DAVIDSON HOUSE

**Constructed:** 1908
**Address:** 57 Tillinghast Place, Buffalo, New York

The house embodies a more architecturally complex example of Wright's Prairie Style, and the marked horizontal emphasis has been further elongated so that interior spaces seem to nestle deeper within the building. It is accessed by discreet entrances, which are not altogether obvious in their placement. The Davidson house is, again, of cruciform plan, and boasts a large and open-plan, two-story living area on the interior, enclosed on the exterior by a double elevation of glass set within tall vertical panels, which rise from the stylobate to beneath the eaves. The house is typical of Wright's Prairie Style, although perhaps more spreading than some other examples.

ABOVE: The low, spreading walls of the structure are highly sculptural in their varied movement toward and away from the mass of the building. The house almost seems to emerge from within the site, rather than resting upon its surface. Dark bands, which delineate separate floors and surfaces run almost unbroken, echoing the natural expanse of landscape, although the building was constructed within a mainly urban setting.

## ISABEL ROBERTS (ROBERTS-SCOTT) HOUSE

**Constructed:** 1908
**Address:** 603 Edgewood Place, River Forest, Illinois

Hanks noted that Isabel Roberts was Wright's secretary at Oak Park. She also appears to have been the daughter of Charles E. Roberts, who commissioned Wright on two occasions in 1896 for the remodeling of his residence in Oak Park and the stables located behind. The Roberts-Scott residence is a Prairie house of cruciform plan. Wright himself carried out remodeling of the house in 1955 for the subsequent owner Warren Scott, employing a brick veneer for resurfacing the exterior. The central wing of the facade is faced with wood board that delineates three vertical, floor-to-ceiling "panels" of sub-divided glazing. Behind these lies a double-height living area reminiscent of other Prairie house interiors, although in this case the interior plan is stepped in three levels. It has functional spaces a half level below the first story, the living area on the ground story, and the bedrooms a half level above that. The arrangement of living space inside the house is not entirely clearly delineated by the treatment of the facade.

ABOVE: The stylobate has been extended forward to create a low lying planting box, whose contour is organically fixed to the overall composition of the house. Uniquely, Wright constructed the south porch around an existing tree, wrapping the shallow pitch of the low-hung roof around the trunk, which grows up from inside the porch.

# J. H. AMBERG HOUSE

**Constructed:** 1909
**Address:** 505 College Avenue, South East, Grand Rapids, Michigan

The design of this house has been criticized as somewhat disproportionate, and it has therefore been suggested that Wright's participation in executing the commission was perhaps negligible. David Hanks pointed out that Wright's assistant Hermann van Holst took over responsibility for the commission, which remained in the drafting stages when Wright left for Europe in 1909. Wright's gifted draughtswoman Marian Mahoney appears to have, at least in part, taken charge of the designing stages. Hanks, however, uncovered no documentation to prove designs for the Amberg house, interior or exterior, could be firmly attributed to her.

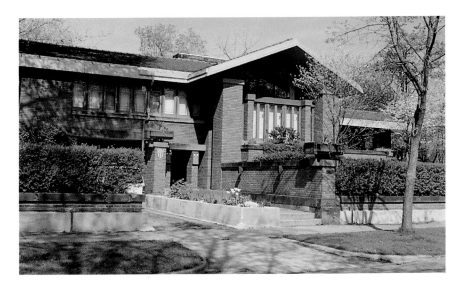

ABOVE: The horizontal brick courses of the facing are a characteristically Wrightian motif, as are the use of the plinth above the entryway, and the double-elevation glazing of the central wing of the facade.

# FRANK J. BAKER HOUSE

**Constructed:** 1909

**Address:** 507 Lake Avenue, Wilmette, Illinois

The Baker residence is remarkably like Wright's home for Isabel Roberts, in that it is also a Prairie house of cruciform plan on the ground floor. It differs in that the interior space extends to the full height of the windows and is not on two levels. The exterior organization of the building reveals, rather than disguises, the organization of interior space. The porches which extend laterally are both single story, although the extensive use of glazing diminishes the impact of their wood and plaster construction.

RIGHT: This design, like that of the house for Isabel Roberts, shows a cleaner, less decorative and more modern architectural expression than many of Wright's previous Prairie houses, which were more earthy and visibly "organic" in their overall effect. Here, "organicism" seems to have been moderated by the aesthetic purity of modernity.

# GEORGE C. STEWART HOUSE

**Constructed:** 1909
**Address:** 196 Hot Springs Road, Montecito, California

Scholars of Wright's work have pointed out that the Stewart residence is effectively the transmission of the Prairie house model to California's northern coast. The architectural model, however, is notably sympathetic to the environment of the north Pacific area. This was the very first of Wright's houses to be built in California, and possesses all the typical characteristics of the Prairie Style. This includes the low-lying structural format, the ground plan, the organisation of interior space, and the motif of the two-story living area behind a glass frontage.

ABOVE: The dramatic impact of Wright's use of unusually broad, extending eaves beneath a low gabled roof line is clearly visible in this house. A covered veranda partially hidden beneath the volume of the second story confirms Wright's vision of the domestic residence as a secure domain in which the need for privacy is expressed through architectural form.

LEFT: Wright's use of redwood siding on the Stewart residence produces a rich textural play across the surfaces of the building, and attests to his philosophy of incorporating native, indigenous materials into every project. The deep hues of the siding blend evocatively into the local landscape, giving the property the unique character of California's Pacific Coast.

# OSCAR B. BALCH HOUSE

**Constructed:** 1911
**Address:** 611 North Kenilworth Avenue, Oak Park, Illinois

In its basic format the house is clearly modeled on Wright's Prairie Style, but perhaps lacking the architectural finesse of a thoroughly Wrightian design. It is wood-trimmed and plaster-rendered in the dark against light pattern characteristic of Wright but has, like the Amberg house, been criticized for being disproportionate and not entirely the result of Wright's personal intervention in the commission. Certainly by 1911, Wright had been in Europe for two years, and the project had been finalized by his studio.

ABOVE: The two-story frontal bay provides a strong vertical accent to the otherwise elongated, horizontal design of the house. The building marks the mature phase of Wright's Prairie Style. It is a thoroughly unified composition of square and rectangular forms, which effortlessly flow into one another. Less significant areas are organically linked to the more ambitious, broader forms of the building.

# HARRY S. ADAMS HOUSE

**Constructed:** 1913
**Address:** 710 Augusta Avenue, Oak Park, Illinois

Delightful variation in the depth of the facade give this house a sculptural complexity clearly of Wright's own making. His final domestic design to be constructed in Oak Park, the house has been said to represent a summation of Wright's Prairie Style. Concrete plinths and stylobates are set in contrast to running brick courses and wood trim, while the progressive forward movement of the asymmetrical facade shows Wright at his best as a designer of architectural surfaces. The proportions are thoroughly convincing, and the casement windows create sophisticated plays of light and dark both on the interior and exterior of the house.

ABOVE: An outstanding example of Wright's fully developed Prairie Style, the Adams residence shows all the subtle textural and surface variations, which make Wright's interpretation of the Prairie Style so significant. The plan is longitudinal, with interior rooms organized progressively along that axis.

# INDEX AND FURTHER READING

Frank Lloyd Wright: *An Autobiography* (1932; reprinted
   in Frank Lloyd Wright Collected Writings, New York, 1992)

Norris Kelly Smith: Frank Lloyd Wright: *A Study in Architectural
   Content* (Englewood Cliffs, New Jersey, 1966)

William Allin Storrer: *The Architecture of Frank Lloyd Wright,
   a Complete Catalogue* (Cambridge, Massachusetts, 1974)

David A. Hanks: *The Decorative Designs of Frank Lloyd Wright*
   (New York, 1979)